UnDebted

A Blueprint for Conquering Debt Addiction

Priscilla Na

TABLE OF CONTENT

INTRODUCTION

Hello there!

Let me guess: you're here because you have a severe debt problem. Were you embarrassed by the sentence? When I initially encountered that truth, I cringed.

Debt!

This one-syllable word has caused great people's fall and many families' disintegration. I speak from first-hand experience.

Debt addiction is a quiet illness that affects millions of people in the world of personal finance. Similar to how substance abuse may eat away at a person's health, debt is capable of eating away at their mental and emotional stability as well as their financial stability. Everyone, regardless of their socioeconomic status, occupation, or family history, is affected by the pervasive debt addiction epidemic.

In addition, more and more people are getting into debt due to the allure of quick cash from loans and credit cards. Because it's so easy to rack up debt, we tend to ignore the repercussions that will befall us in the future. When people are burdened with debt, it affects more than just their bank accounts. It causes emotional distress, disrupts sleep, and strains relationships.

As I indicated, it has wreaked havoc on people's minds and shattered families. This reality has amplified the importance of eliminating debt.

Getting out of debt is crucial to regain control of your finances. A mountain of debt can engulf your life, preventing you from living the life you want and casting a shadow over your prospects. Eliminating debt goes beyond being fiscally responsible; it's about reclaiming the power to choose your fate and live the life you want.

In the following chapters of "UnDebted", we set out on a life-altering adventure. As important as establishing a budget and reducing spending, this method takes a more comprehensive approach by tackling the underlying issues that lead to debt addiction and providing a road map for long-term recovery. Following the steps outlined in UnDebted, you can overcome your debts and develop an attitude conducive to financial abundance and freedom.

Taking charge, escaping debt, and living life to the fullest are all necessary steps in achieving financial independence. However, you should know that you are not alone as we explore the complexities of debt addiction and its far-reaching effects. Insights, practical tools, and a road map to a future free of debt and empowered are all here in this book, which will be your trusted friend on your journey.

Welcome to the UnDebted journey. See you on the other side,

Priscilla Na

CHAPTER ONE

Understanding Debt Addiction

One dangerous trap stands out in the maze of personal fin ance, where financial decisions impact our lives— debt addiction.

Why is debt a global problem at the individual, business, and governmental levels? From the beginning of human interaction, some portion of every community's wealth has always been owed.

However, a more

considerable percentage of the population is in debt nowa days, and it's nearly never for a good reason.

Unraveling the mysteries of this terrible occurrence is the first step in achieving financial freedom.

Defining Debt Addiction

When people are addicted to debt, it goes beyond simple financial irresponsibility. The problem lies more with an unhealthy and compulsive relationship with borrowing than just amassing debt. "Living today on what you expect to earn in the future" is one definition of going into debt.

Addiction to debt is characterized by a pattern of behavior in which people seek momentary relief through spending, only to get trapped in an endless cycle of debt. It is an unhealthy dependence on credit and loans to satisfy emotional and psychological demands.

It is believed that there are three leading causes of people's debt:

a. Ignorance, which means they didn't know better and couldn't do better, rendering them helpless.
b. Greed or selfishness leads individuals to succumb to advertising and satisfy their desires by living beyond their means. Such people aren't willing to live in, drive, or wear what they can afford.
c. Tragedies that cause undeserved hardship, such as illness, betrayal, or theft.

Focusing on debt addiction, we will examine areas a and b psychologically while proposing remedies for these three areas.

Recognizing that there is a deeper relationship between one's emotional health and financial decisions is essential to understanding debt addiction, which goes beyond the simple act of borrowing. Identifying the subtle signs of debt addiction, learning where it comes from, and making a plan to overcome it are the first steps toward recovery.

Recognizing the Signs and Symptoms

The same telltale signals characterize the debt addiction trail as any other addiction. The symptoms could include anything from excessive spending to persistent worry about money. It is critical to recognize these signs to break the vicious cycle of debt.

The use of credit to pretend to be wealthy, an inability to control spending, and keeping financial decisions a secret from loved ones are all symptoms that may be present. Any negative or positive emotional reaction to a transaction, such as remorse, humiliation, or joy, should be taken seriously. One can take action toward liberation from debt addiction by becoming more adept at recognizing these indicators.

How Debt Addiction Affects Your Life

A person's life is affected in many ways by their debt addiction, which goes beyond just their finances. When money worries follow you everywhere you go, they cast a shadow over your personal life, professional goals, and your health in general.

Debt addiction fundamentally changes decision-making, making choices motivated by short-term satisfaction rather than long-term security. As a result, relationships may experience tension as daily financial challenges become more apparent. When people are weighed down by debt, they are less likely to take advantage of chances and advance in their careers.

The mental health consequences of being overly indebted can include increased anxiety, sadness, and stress. Every waking moment is usually consumed by financial responsibilities, which makes it hard to sleep, lowers self-esteem, and lowers life quality generally.

If you want to escape the grip of debt addiction, you must first understand how it impacts your life. Gaining a deep understanding of how it affects your emotional, mental, and relational health will enable you to take charge of your financial recovery by making deliberate choices.

In the chapters that follow, we will examine the complexities of debt addiction in further detail, looking at ways to escape its clutches and establish a solid financial footing again. Now is the moment to face the darkness and start living without debt.

CHAPTER TWO

The Psychology of Debts

An examination of the psychology of debt sheds light on the intricate web of relationships between our feelings, actions, and choices as they pertain to our financial futures. To solve the ambiguities of our financial decisions, it is crucial to comprehend the mental foundations of debt.

Exploring the Emotional and Psychological Aspects

Debt is more than a number; it carries many feelings and subtleties in psychology. By delving into debt's mental and emotional underpinnings, we can better understand the reasoning and patterns of thought that drive financial decision-making.

When people are emotionally distressed, many resort to taking out loans. In the short term, it might alleviate tension, worry, or the need for immediate satisfaction. To know what motivates people financially, we must get to the bottom of their emotional attachments to debt. People can learn to cope with difficult emotions better, free from the weight of debt if they recognize and work through these feelings.

Identifying Triggers and Compulsive Spending

Many people get into a vicious cycle of compulsive spending due to a combination of factors that set them on the path to debt addiction. To uncover these causes of hasty financial decisions is to shine a light on the darkness.

The influence of advertising, fears, and social pressures to maintain a specific appearance are just a few examples of the many potential triggers. Sales, discounts, and the thrill of making a purchase can attract people and lead to compulsive buying. The first step in breaking the habit of impulsive spending and learning to be more deliberate with one's money is identifying what sets off these episodes.

How Debt Addiction is Different from Healthy Debt

Differentiating between manageable debt and the path to debt addiction is critical. Acquiring debt with a well-planned repayment strategy might help you achieve your financial goals, like buying a home or paying for college. Debt addiction, on the other hand, is characterized by an irrational and compulsive need to borrow money.

Anyone aiming for financial wellness would do well to familiarize themselves with this difference. To do this, one must change their perspective on debt from an emotional crutch to a strategic tool for achieving financial security. With this new outlook, you may finally free yourself from debt addiction and start planning your money purposefully.

As we further explore the mental aspects of debt, we will find ways to retrain our brains to think differently, control our emotions, and have a positive connection with money. People can begin a life-changing path toward financial wellness and freedom from debt addiction by understanding the psychological components of debt.

CHAPTER THREE

The Consequences of Debt Addiction

Debt addiction has far-reaching effects that go well beyond the bottom line as it entangles our lives. Anyone hoping to escape the clutches of debt addiction and start the path to financial freedom would do well to familiarize themselves with the many effects of this addiction.

Financial Consequences: Debt Spiral and Interest Rates

The monetary fallout is one of the most obvious effects of being addicted to debt. The debt spiral is a never-ending cycle of taking out loans to pay off current debts. Eventually, the load becomes too much to bear. An already tolerable debt becomes an insurmountable mountain when interest rates are added. Albert Einstein said, "Compound interest is the world's eighth wonder. Those who understand it earn it… those who don't, pay it."

Interest payments eat away at hard-earned money as debt builds up, taking resources that could be put to better use elsewhere. The effects hit hard on one's financial security, lowering credit ratings, cutting off future chances, and trapping one in a never-ending cycle of over-reliance on credit.

To inspire people to take bold action and escape the vicious cycle of debt, it is critical to comprehend how interest rates work and the debt spiral.

Emotional and Mental Impacts

Addiction to debt has devastating effects on one's emotional and mental health in addition to the more obvious monetary costs. Worry, despair, and a generalized feeling of powerlessness can set in when money worries and the prospect of debt always hang over one's head.

The decision-making process isn't the only part of life where emotions are involved; they permeate every part. The continual stress of managing payments can diminish an individual's quality of life, the terror of receiving calls from creditors, and the restless nights spent worrying about one's financial destiny. Prioritizing mental health and building resilience amid financial hardship requires acknowledging the emotional toll.

Strained Relationships and Social Isolations

Isolation from loved ones is a common symptom of debt addiction, as it is with other addictions. Disagreements about spending habits, financial opacity, or failure to contribute to shared financial goals are common causes of strained relationships with friends and family.

People who are struggling with debt often avoid social situations because they feel ashamed or embarrassed, which can lead to social isolation. Having trouble forming meaningful connections and dealing with the emotional toll of debt addiction can be made worse by the fear of judgment and the perceived shame that comes with financial troubles.

When trying to mend fences and encourage open dialogue, it's essential to acknowledge the effect that debt has on relationships. Recovering from a debt addiction is a journey that requires the understanding and support of people closest to us, not just ourselves.

We will discuss ways to lessen the impact of financial difficulties, put our mental health first, and repair relationships as we face the aftereffects of debt addiction. When people know all the potential outcomes, they can better plan for their financial recovery and build a life free from debt.

CHAPTER FOUR
Assessing Your Debt Situation

Taking an honest and open stock of your financial situation is crucial before starting the path to financial independence. Assessing your current debt situation is essential to reducing debt and achieving financial freedom.

Taking Stock of Your Debt

Recognizing that you have debt is the first step in dealing with it directly. It would be best if you first inventoried all your monetary commitments to take stock of your debts. This encompasses several types of debt, such as unpaid loans, credit card bills, mortgage payments, and more. Please include all your creditors, the amount you owe them, the interest rates they charge, and the monthly payment due dates.

You must be completely honest with yourself through this process, no matter how painful. You can only make educated decisions or devise effective plans to reduce your debt once you accept the truth about your financial status.

Creating a Detailed Debt Inventory

Making a thorough inventory is the next step after figuring out what you owe. You can better understand your financial situation by organizing your debts. Divide the high-interest debts from the low-interest ones and put them in separate categories. This inventory will be your guide as you work to reduce your debt.

Outline relevant terms and conditions, including minimum monthly payments and due dates. Prioritizing debts strategically and adapting your strategy to each obligation's unique features are made possible by a well-organized and transparent inventory.

Calculating Your Debt-to-Income Ratio

The debt-to-income ratio is essential to consider while analyzing your financial position. How much of your income goes toward paying off debt can be better understood with this ratio.

To find it, divide your gross monthly income by the total amount of your monthly loan payments. The resultant percentage makes it easy to see how much of your salary goes toward paying off debt.

One possible indicator of financial distress is a high debt-to-income ratio, which shows a more significant debt load. Knowing this ratio is essential to assess your financial health and find places where changes are possible. You want to reduce this ratio as you pay off your debt to have more money for savings, investments, and fun.

This in-depth analysis of your financial status will serve as the basis for developing a tailored strategy to reduce your debt in the upcoming chapters. You must know where you stand financially before you can embark on freedom. Doing so will give you the agency to make educated choices and set you up for a future free of debt.

CHAPTER FIVE
Setting Clear Financial Goals

The road to financial independence can be navigated with the help of well-defined and manageable objectives. Set goals to get out of debt and build a lifelong financial safety net. They will show you the way and give you something to work toward.

The Importance of Setting Goals

Achieving your financial goals provides purpose and guidance along the way. In doing so, they concretize the intangible goal of financial independence. Reducing debt can feel like a never-ending maze if you don't have any specific objectives.

Having monetary objectives gives one direction and purpose in life. Every goal you reach, whether paying off a certain amount of debt, building an emergency fund, or investing for the future, is a milestone you can celebrate. The ability to make well-informed financial decisions that align with your aims is greatly enhanced by having clear goals to work toward.

Short-Term and Long-Term Financial Objectives

Striking a balance between immediate and distant goals is essential for productive goal-setting. You can keep yourself motivated with short-term goals since you can immediately see the results of your efforts. Some examples are lowering the balance on a high-interest loan, building a little emergency fund, or paying off a credit card.

Conversely, long-term objectives provide a picture of your financial future. Goals like this include eliminating all credit card debt, putting money down for a house down payment, or creating a comfortable nest egg for retirement. To create a safe and prosperous future for yourself and your loved ones, it is vital to have clear and attainable long-term objectives.

A dynamic and long-term plan for financial success is born from the harmony of short-term and long-term goals. While short-term achievements are a source of motivation, the long-term vision keeps you engaged in the journey.

Visualizing a Debt-Free Future

Visualizing the process is a potent tool for achieving one's objectives. The ability to see a future free of debt influences one's attitude and actions in the present. With your eyes closed, imagine a world where debt is no longer a burden, you may make free choices, and opportunities abound.

Making a mental plan for a future without debt will help you stay motivated and on track. It is a motivating reminder of the final goal in the face of adversity. Instead of passively wishing for something, you might actively work for it through visualization.

Moving through the following chapters, we will build a customized strategy to help you reduce your debt based on your objectives. They will be the engine that keeps you going, making your dreams and goals a reality while keeping you from debt.

CHAPTER SIX
Creating a Debt-Reduction Plan

Now that you know what you want from life financially, it's time to implement your plans. A debt reduction plan is an organized way to free oneself from the burden of debt that requires careful planning, setting priorities, and implementing a strategy.

Strategies for Tackling Debt

A systematic handling of your financial responsibilities is the first step towards successfully reducing debt. Several tried-and-true methods can be used, and they all address distinct economic scenarios:

Debt Snowball: In the debt snowball strategy, you pay the minimum on more extensive obligations while focusing on paying off smaller ones. We pay off the lowest debt first and then go on to the next smallest one. With each loan paid off, the snowball effect builds, and you'll feel better and better about yourself.

Debt Avalanche: The avalanche technique, on the other hand, ranks loans according to interest rates. To save the most money on interest over time, prioritize paying off the debt with the highest interest rate first. A snowball effect occurs when you first pay off the debt with the highest interest rate.

Debt Consolidation: Are you borrowing more money than you need? Consider consolidating your debts into one smaller loan to make payments easier and save money on interest. One way to accomplish this is by switching to a low-interest credit card or getting a debt consolidation loan.

Negotiating with Creditors: Creditors might be approached to seek assistance by negotiating reduced interest rates, longer repayment terms, or settlement offers. If you are having financial difficulties, many creditors are prepared to collaborate to discover a solution that works for both of you.

Before deciding on a strategy, consider your financial situation, personal preferences, and long-term objectives.

Combining these strategies for a more thorough strategy to reduce debt is also possible.

Prioritizing High-Interest Debts

Pay off your high-interest loans first when planning to reduce your debt. Credit card balances, payday loans, and other forms of high-interest debt can quickly build up and impede monetary advancement. Paying off these high-interest debts first will reduce your overall interest expense and free up capital for other, more strategic uses.

Find out which bills have the highest interest rates and put more money toward paying them off faster. By narrowing your focus, you can reduce the total cost of debt and speed up your path to financial independence.

Snowball vs. Avalanche Method

Your financial mentality and tastes will play a role in deciding between the snowball and avalanche approaches. By rapidly paying off smaller debts, the snowball method provides psychological gains, which improve motivation. On the other hand, Avalanche methods maximize economic efficiency, resulting in more significant long-term savings on interest payments.

Before settling on a strategy, consider your financial personality and what drives you. The snowball method could work wonders if being motivated and enjoying small wins is paramount. The avalanche method is the way to achieve your goals of optimizing for long-term financial savings.

The following chapters will focus on the specifics of putting your debt reduction plan into action, with detailed explanations of each method and instructions on how to implement them. Remember that getting out from under your debt is a long haul, not a quick fix, and having a solid strategy will be your rock along the way.

CHAPTER SEVEN
Budgeting and Financial Discipline

Budgeting is essential to handle one's finances wisely. Achieving financial independence and overcoming debt addiction necessitate the creation of a practical budget to direct spending, generate savings, and methodically decrease debt.

Establishing a Realistic Budget

Rather than being an oppressive collection of regulations, a reasonable budget can serve as a guide that helps you make deliberate and educated choices about your money. The first step is to sort your cash coming in and going out. Allocate a part for discretionary expenditures after prioritizing critical requirements like housing, utilities, and groceries.

When making a budget, balancing paying for necessities, setting aside money for savings, and paying off debt is essential. Use a budgeting tool or app to monitor your spending and ensure your budget aligns with your financial objectives. You should periodically examine and revise your budget as your financial condition changes.

Cutting Unnecessary Expenses

As you review your spending plan, look for places to save money without sacrificing your necessities or health. A careful eye and the determination to put long-term financial goals ahead of temporary pleasures are crucial for cutting wasteful spending.

It may be worthwhile to evaluate your patterns of subscription services, eating out, and impulsive purchasing. Try to get better utility rates or look into other, less expensive options. You can save a lot of money by making small changes in several places, and then you can use that money to pay off your debt or put money aside for an emergency.

Building an Emergency Fund

Being financially disciplined involves more than just paying off debt; it also consists of saving up for the unexpected. To weather economic storms, it is essential to have an emergency reserve. An emergency fund can be a lifesaver when faced with unanticipated costs, such as a loss of income or severe illness.

Begin with a tiny target, like saving enough money to cover one month's costs, and work your way up to saving enough to cover three to six months. Thanks to this emergency reserve, you won't have to use credit as much in an emergency, and your debt repayment will continue unabated.

Discipline in handling money is essential for sticking to a budget and paying off debt. Achieving financial independence requires deliberate decision-making, a laser-like focus on objectives, and the development of habits that will propel you forward. The chapters will delve into practical tactics for staying disciplined with your finances, conquering obstacles, and commemorating achievements as you strive for long-term economic prosperity.

CHAPTER EIGHT

Increasing Income

Raising your income is a potent weapon in the fight against debt and toward financial independence, complementing the importance of spending control and budgeting. If you want to get a head start on paying off your debt and saving money, this chapter will show you how to increase your earnings.

Exploring Additional Income Sources

Improving your financial situation might be as simple as diversifying your revenue sources. Looking for ways to supplement your income can take many shapes and sizes, from more conventional job openings to riskier business pursuits. Think about these options:

- **Part-Time Employment:** Look for temporary or part-time jobs that fit your schedule and talents.

- **Freelancing:** Offering your skills as a freelance writer, graphic designer, consultant, or in any other area is a great way to put your knowledge to use.

- **Consulting or Coaching:** Offering in-person or virtual consulting or coaching services is a great way to use your expertise and experience.

- **Investing:** Look into stocks, real estate, and bond investments that can yield passive income, such as dividends or interest.

Side Hustles and Gig Economy Opportunities

The proliferation of the "gig economy" has made it easier than ever to start a side business. An extra source of income, more freedom, and the chance to make money doing something you love are all benefits of pursuing a side hustle. Some everyday side hustles are:

- **Ride-sharing or Delivery Services:** You can make more money by using ridesharing or delivery services like Uber or Lyft or by delivering meals.

- **Freelance Platforms:** Post your services and expertise on Upwork, Fiverr, or TaskRabbit and reach customers worldwide.

- **Online Selling:** Use marketplaces like Etsy, eBay, or Amazon to provide unique wares, antiques, and handcrafted goods.

- **Content Creation:** Think about using sites like Medium, YouTube, or Patreon to make money off of your writing, photography, or video-producing skills.

Negotiating a Raise or Promotion

You can directly enhance your salary at your current job by negotiating a raise or pursuing a promotion. Showcase your contributions to the company, showcase your talents and achievements, and investigate industry compensation standards to prepare for such conversations. Be self-assured and know your worth to the firm before you walk into these conversations.

Increase your salary, job satisfaction, and career trajectory by starting conversations about career advancement. Make a calculated effort to prove that you are valuable to your company and worthy of a raise.

In the following chapters, we will discuss how to properly handle a rise in income, ensuring that the extra cash helps you reach your financial objectives, such as paying off debt and amassing wealth. You may empower yourself to accelerate your path to financial independence by carefully boosting your income.

CHAPTER NINE
Overcoming Emotional Challenges

Achieving financial independence is a personal and emotional quest, not just a question of statistics and tactics. Emotional difficulties sometimes accompany debt reduction and financial stability; Chapter 9 examines these challenges and offers information on navigating and overcoming them.

Dealing with Shame and Guilt

Feelings of shame and guilt often accompany debt for many people. No matter what caused the debt to accumulate—unforeseen events or poor decisions—these emotions can be crippling. Conquering feelings of guilt and shame:

- **Self-Compassion:** Recognize that you, too, will encounter financial difficulties. Take care of yourself, and remember that you are more than the sum of your mistakes.

- **Acceptance:** Recognize your financial condition as it is without passing judgment. Embracing change begins with acceptance.

- **Learn and Grow:** Take advantage of every situation as a chance to learn and grow. Accept the lessons that money problems can teach you and resolve to make wise choices moving forward.

Coping with Anxiety and Stress

Mental and emotional health can suffer when people are under financial strain. Stress over money, expenses, and what's to come may take over a person's life. Here are some techniques for coping:

- **Break Down Goals:** If you're overwhelmed by the sheer magnitude of your financial goals, try breaking them down into smaller, more achievable tasks.

- **Mindfulness and Relaxation Techniques:** Stress management and being in the here and now are both helped by regular relaxation techniques like deep breathing, meditation, or mindfulness.

- **Seek Professional Help:** If your worry worsens, it may be time to see a mental health expert or financial advisor. Depending on your unique circumstances, they can offer personalized advice and assistance.

Seeking Support from Loved Ones

Sharing financial difficulties can make them easier to bear. If you need help, talk to someone you care about or join a support group. If you want to get to know someone better and get good advice or insights, try being more open with them. To promote fruitful dialogues:

- **Be Honest and Transparent:** Always tell the truth about your financial situation, including your objectives, obstacles, and achievements. Being open and honest helps establish credibility and garners backing.

- **Establish Limits:** Make Your Needs and Expectations Known. One aspect is discussing ways people can help you without encouraging lousy money habits.

- **Educate and Involve:** If it's okay with them, teach your loved ones about money management. The better their understanding, the more effective their support can be.

To stay resilient on your journey to financial freedom, you must acknowledge and handle emotional obstacles. To strengthen yourself against the emotional challenges of the journey, it is helpful to have a good outlook, reach out for assistance, and use efficient coping methods. The following chapters discuss staying motivated and disciplined and celebrating big and small wins.

CHAPTER TEN

Staying on Track

As the complexities of your debt reduction path become apparent, it becomes critical to maintain motivation, discipline, and adaptability. The tenth chapter delves into methods for maintaining focus, acknowledging achievements, and overcoming obstacles to financial independence.

Maintaining Motivation and Discipline

Being self-aware and having a strategy can help you maintain the drive and discipline you need to reduce your debt successfully. Here are some suggestions:

- **Set Milestones:** Make a plan to reduce your debt and divide it into smaller, more manageable goals. Keep motivation high by celebrating each milestone.

- **Visualize Your Success:** Remind yourself often that you are working towards your goal of financial independence. Motivate yourself by visualizing a future free of debt.

- **Remind Yourself of Goals:** Post a conspicuous reminder of your financial goals. Revisiting your objectives frequently will help you remain focused, whether using a vision board, a written list, or a digital reminder.

- **Stay Accountable:** Share your objectives with someone you trust—a family member, close friend, or financial advisor—so they can encourage you and keep you on track.

Celebrating Small Wins

It is crucial to commemorate minor successes while you work toward significant financial objectives. Positive thinking and reinforcement of success are fostered by acknowledging and enjoying every victory, no matter how small:

- **Create a Reward System:** Determine how you will reward yourself when reaching certain financial milestones. Any positive reinforcement, like a little treat or some free time, would do.

- **Reflect on Progress:** Make it a habit to regularly take stock of how far you've come. Keep track of the money you've saved, the debts you've paid off, and any good financial habits you've established.

- **Share Achievements:** Tell your loved ones or a group that will encourage you about your financial successes. Receiving praise from others might make you feel even better about yourself.

Adapting to Unexpected Financial Challenges

Unanticipated obstacles may emerge, and financial journeys are rarely smooth. Being adaptable and proactive is critical when faced with these challenges:

- **Emergency Fund Utilization:** If you're saving money for a rainy day, put some of it to good use to handle unexpected costs without letting your debt reduction plan go by the wayside.

- **Reassess and Adjust Goals:** When faced with unforeseen obstacles, it's essential to reevaluate your financial goals and make any necessary adjustments to your timetables or priorities. Adaptability is guaranteed by goal-setting flexibility.

- **Consider Consulting an Expert:** If problems continue, consulting an expert in financial planning or counseling may be helpful. Based on your specific situation, they can devise tailored methods and recommendations.

- **Change Your Thinking:** Instead of seeing problems as insurmountable barriers, try viewing them as temporary setbacks. To be financially resilient, one must have an optimistic outlook and be open to change.

Your will to achieve financial independence will be strengthened by keeping yourself motivated, acknowledging achievements, and adjusting to unforeseen obstacles. You have shown remarkable perseverance and resolve by remaining focused. As you reach your debt reduction and financial objectives, we will go into the following chapters to help you understand how everything comes together.

CHAPTER ELEVEN

Building a Debt-Free Future

In Chapter 11, you will learn how to go from debt to having a financially stable future near the end of your debt-reduction journey. Topics covered in this chapter include long-term financial planning, short-term wealth creation, and investing for the future.

Achieving Your Financial Goals

Although paying off your debt is a huge accomplishment, you still have a long way to go on your financial journey. The moment has come to establish fresh objectives that are in harmony with your hope for a prosperous and satisfying future:

- **Set New Goals:** Think About What You Want to Achieve Now and in the Future. Outline your new financial objectives: homeownership, further education, business startup, or early retirement.

- **Raising Your Emergency Fund:** Save enough money to last three to six months of living costs in an emergency. This will make sure that there is a substantial financial safety net in case something unexpected happens.

- **Explore Lifestyle Upgrades:** Take a look at chances to modify your lifestyle to reflect your beliefs and goals as your financial condition improves.

Strategies for Building Wealth

Once you free yourself from debt, you can put your energy into accumulating wealth and planning for your financial future. Investigate realistic methods for amassing riches:

- **Budgeting for Savings:** Set aside a portion of your money every paycheck. Building money begins with regular savings, whether for immediate needs (like a trip) or more distant ones (like retirement).

- **Debt Avoidance:** Stay away from unneeded debt by changing your thinking. It would be best to use caution when taking on additional financial obligations, even though some may be strategic (like a mortgage with a low interest rate, for example).

- **Continuous Learning:** Maintain a state of perpetual learning by keeping abreast of developments in personal finance, investing, and wealth creation. When you have all the necessary information, you can make intelligent choices to help your financial situation.

Investing for the Future

The ability to invest in one's financial future is a vital component of a comfortable retirement. Here are some financial strategies to explore as you work towards a future free of debt:

- **Diversification:** To lessen the impact of potential losses, diversify your holdings across various asset classes. Stocks, bonds, property, and other investment vehicles can all be part of a diversified portfolio.

- **Retirement Savings:** Regularly put money away in a retirement account (401(k) or IRA). Looking at other tax-advantaged savings choices besides employer-sponsored retirement plans would be best.

- **Professional Advice:** Seek the counsel of a financial advisor to help you develop an investing plan that considers your objectives, level of comfort with risk, and time horizon.

Achieving financial independence is about getting from point A to point B; it's about making a life for oneself that can withstand the test of time. You may ensure your financial legacy as you enter this new chapter by keeping your financial goals in mind, making educated decisions, and utilizing wealth-building tactics. Next, we'll go into managing your wealth, creating a financial strategy, and reaching your long-term goals.

CHAPTER TWELVE
Life After Debt

Reaching the pinnacle of a debt-free life is a transformative accomplishment. This Chapter explores the myriad possibilities that unfold after debt freedom, emphasizing the freedom of debt-free living, setting new financial goals, and the potential to empower others on their journey to break free from debt addiction.

The Freedom of Debt-Free Living

A tremendous sense of emancipation comes with being free of debt. Now that your financial options are unrestricted, a universe of possibilities awaits you:

- **Financial Flexibility:** Rather than worrying about paying off debt, the ability to spend your money any way you like is a critical component of financial flexibility. Take pleasure in the freedom to act by your beliefs and goals.

- **Reduced Stress:** Having debt is a continual source of anxiety for many people. Reduce the strain on your mental and emotional health caused by mounting debt.

- **Enhanced Quality of Life:** You can now enjoy a higher quality of life by redirecting the previously used resources to pay off debt to experiences, personal growth, and activities that offer you joy and fulfillment.

Setting New Financial Goals

Now that you have a clean slate in terms of your financial future, you can create new objectives that reflect your changing desires:

- **Advanced Education:** Invest in your skills and expertise by pursuing additional education or professional development to grow your career and increase your earning potential.

- **Homeownership:** If you are considering purchasing a home, whether it's your first or an upgrade to suit your evolving needs, it's essential to consider the financial implications.

- **Generational Wealth:** Look into ways to leave a legacy of money. This involves teaching the next generation about money management, investing in assets with potential appreciation over time, and carefully preparing one's estate.

Helping Others Break Free from Debt Addiction

People going through the same things can learn much from your story of getting out of debt. You can make a difference by assisting other people in overcoming their debt:

- **Share Your Story:** True stories can inspire those going through tough times because they speak directly to the experiences of the tellers.

- **Educate and Advocate:** Get the word out about the dangers of debt addiction and how to get your finances back on track. To equip people to make educated decisions, advocating for financial literacy programs in schools and communities is essential.

- **Mentorship:** Help others who are embarking on the path to debt reduction by offering to be a mentor to them. Help people deal with financial difficulties' emotional and practical aspects.

As you embark on a journey out of debt, remember that you can improve not just your own life but also the lives of those around you. If you can overcome debt addiction, your story will inspire those fighting for freedom. In the last chapters, we will consider financial wellness more comprehensively, looking at how it relates to individual happiness, community, and society at large.

CONCLUSION

Embracing the Path to Financial Freedom

As you stand at the threshold of financial freedom, take a moment to reflect on the remarkable journey you've undertaken. The chapters you've traversed, the challenges you've overcome, and the victories you've celebrated all contribute to a narrative of resilience, growth, and transformation.

Embracing Financial Freedom

As you step into financial freedom, embrace the newfound possibilities and opportunities that await. Your financial choices are no longer constrained by the weight of debt, allowing you to design a life that aligns with your values and aspirations. This freedom is not just about the absence of debt but the empowerment to make intentional choices that contribute to your overall well-being.

Encouragement for a Debt-Free Life

Everything you need to get out of debt and succeed in the financial wellness environment is in the chapters you've read. As you face the challenges of life after debt, remember to apply the skills of discipline, resilience, and financial knowledge. Share your wisdom and experiences to help others overcome their debt addiction and assist them on their path to recovery.

Remember that achieving financial independence is a process, not a final goal, as you progress. Learning new things, adjusting to changing circumstances, and starting over with goals that reflect your priorities are all part of the process. Adopting a financially sound lifestyle gives you the power to build a life you love, full of adventures, meaningful work, and satisfaction.

Congratulations on reaching this pivotal moment in your financial journey. May your path to financial freedom inspire others, and the chapters ahead be filled with prosperity, contentment, and the ongoing pursuit of a debt-free and fulfilling life.